Phonetic Storybook 10

th • tch • ABC Code • oor = or

Raceway Step 23

MODERN CURRICULUM PRESS

Pearson Learning Group

Contents

Two of These and Three of Those

By Hetty Hubbard

Illustrated by Diane Palmisciano

Vocabulary Words

1. Roth
2. Smith
3. their
4. them
5. these
6. thick
7. thin
8. things
9. think
10. those

Story Words

11. Ann

12. dishes
13. dried
14. girls
15. handed
16. Hello
17. pay day
    payday
18. purse
19. put (po͝ot)
20. slices
21. week

Pam and Ann Smith like
to help. They will make
their beds. Then, they
will help with the dishes.

Today is payday. Pam and Ann will get their pay from Mom.

Pam and Ann waved to Mom. Then, they were off to the store. Their pay was in the little blue purse.

Pam and Ann raced on
their way to the store.
Ann got there first.

There was Mr. Roth.
"Hello, Mr. Roth," Ann
said. "We came to get
some fun things to eat."

"So this is payday
for Pam and Ann," said
Mr. Roth. "What would
you like to buy today?"
he asked.

Ann picked a box of nuts. "I would like one of these, please," she said.

Then, Ann chose some more things. "I will take two of these, and three of those," she said.

Pam put her hand from box to box and said, "I think I will take two boxes of dried cherries and three apples, please."

Pam said, "Let's get some thin slices of cheese for Mom and some figs. She likes them."

"Dad likes thick chunks of cheese and dried apple slices," said Ann. "We can get him those."

Mr. Roth handed each
girl her bag.

"Thank you, Mr. Roth,"
said the girls.

"Thank you," said
Mr. Roth. "I'll see you
next week."

The End

Thad, Theo, and the Cub

By Jean Elsie Cox

Illustrated by Susan Banta

Vocabulary Words

1. both
2. mother
3. Thad
4. Theo
5. thing
6. thump

7. it's
8. nearby
9. Rānger
10. saw
11. slipped

Thad saw it first.
"Look!" said Thad. "What
is that thing?"

"That is a cub!" said
Mom.

"It is little and has thick black fur," said Theo. "I think the cub is cute."

"Do not get near the cub," said Ranger Smith. "It's best to let it be."

"Look!" said Theo. "Now there are three cubs. I see that one cub has left the den. Look! It is near the three rocks by that tree."

"Is the mother nearby?"
asked Thad.

"She may be," said Mom.

Just then, both Thad
and Theo saw the cub try
to go up the tree.

22

All at once, the cub
slipped and fell. The cub
made a little thump.

Then, there was a big thump. What a thump! Thump! Thump!

"It's the mother!" cried Thad.

"Yes," said Ranger Smith. "The mother will take the cubs back into their den. They will be OK. Let's just let them be."

The End

The Baseball Match

By Vida Daly

Illustrated by Marilyn Mets

Vocabulary Words

1. Butch
2. catch
3. catcher

   crutch
4. crutches

5. Gretchen

6. match

7. pitch

8. pitcher

9. pitches

   stitch
10. stitches

11. stretch

12. switch

13. wätch

Story Words

14. 'em

    any time
15. anytime

    be gan
16. began

17. cheering

18. Cindy

19. coach

20 don't

21. faster

22. fence

23. groaned

24. inning

25. innings

26. Kristy

27. least

28. never

no body
29. nobody

30. Oh

31. out

32. outs

prob lem
33. problem

34. score

short stop
35. shortstop

36. smashed

37. strike

38. struck

39. täll

um pire
40. umpire

41. yelling

Two baseball teams were having a match. One team was the Red team. The second team was the Blue team.

The Red team had a
problem. Their catcher
was on crutches. He had
stitches in his leg. The
stitches were under a
bandage.

"We can beat the Blue team, anyway," said the coach. "Kristy, you can catch well. I will switch you to be the first catcher today. You are tall. You can stretch up to catch those pitches."

The game began. One inning went by, then two. Nobody scored. Three, then four innings went by. Still, nobody scored.

Then, the Blue Team was up. Gretchen came to bat.

"Strike one," yelled the umpire, and then, "Strike two!" But then . . .

Watch that ball! It
went over the pitcher.

It went past the
shortstop and into the
back fence!

Gretchen ran to first
base and then past second.

She ran faster to third
and on to home base!

Such cheering and
yelling there was!
"Maybe we will win!"
the Blue team cried.

The Red team had their plans!

"We can't let them beat us," they groaned. "Let's get going!"

"You are up, Kristy!
Let 'em have it!" her
team yelled.

Kristy did! She hit the
very first pitch, and ran
to first base.

Cindy struck out, and so did Mike. Two outs, and Kristy was still stuck on first base!

Then, Butch smashed
one, and Kristy ran all
the way home!

The next batter struck out. Then, it began to rain.

"Oh, no!" said Kristy. "Well, at least the score is tied. When our catcher gets off his crutches, we will finish the game and beat you. Just wait and see!"

"Never!" said the Blue team. "We are a match for you anytime!"

"Don't bet on that!" said Kristy with a smile.

The End

Mitch and His Cat

By Hetty Hubbard

Illustrated by Rosario Valderrama

Vocabulary Words

1. clutch
2. matches
3. Mitch
4. patch
5. snatch
6. stitch

Story Words

7. dash
8. goes
9. jeans
10. lands

11. leaps

12. Mit tens
    Mittens
13. something
14. wänts
    (ŭ)
15. other

Mitch filled a bag with beans. Now he will stitch it up. The bag matches the patch on his blue jeans.

Mitch kicks the bag.
He can switch it from
one leg to the other.

Mitch has a little cat.
Her name is Mittens.
Mittens likes to watch
Mitch play. She thinks
this looks like fun!

Mitch can switch the
bag to his feet. He can
stretch his leg to kick the
bag, but the bag lands
on a patch of grass.

All at once, Mittens makes a dash to snatch the bag away. She can clutch it. Then, she leaps on it.

"Mittens, you are something!" said Mitch. "You can play, too!"

Mitch will play with Mittens. He will pitch the bag to her.

Mittens jumps on it.
"You like this sport,
Mittens," said Mitch.

Mitch gets the bag.
This time, he kicks it
to Mittens.

The bag is sailing to
the top of the shed.
Mittens jumps to get it.
"Oh, no!" said Mitch.
"I can't reach it!"

Mittens wants that bag! She goes up the tree. She leaps to the shed. She can stretch and bat the bag off the shed.

Mitch can catch the bag. "Thank you, Mittens," said Mitch. "You are the best cat ever!"

The End

The ABC Code

By Hetty Hubbard

Illustrations by Maurie Manning

Vocabulary Words

1. anyplace
2. anything
3. Code
4. doing
5. doors
6. fingertips
7. pages
8. Raceway
9. reader
10. sea
11. sorts
12. speeding
13. stories
14. turn
15. unlock

Story Words

16. about
17. books
18. Chart
19. covers
20. know
21. moon
22. open
23. whole
24. words
25. world

By the time you read this story, your Raceway car is speeding on the Raceway Chart to Step 24! Why are you doing this? So you will be a good reader.

When you know the ABC Code, you can use it to unlock words and read stories that tell about all sorts of things.

With the ABC Code, you can read anything you want. You can open doors to anyplace and anything. Those doors are the covers of books!

You do not have to go
to the moon to find out
what is there. You do not
have to go under the sea
to find out what is there.

The whole world is at your fingertips. Turn the pages, and it will open for you.

The End